Powerful Prayers for Every Family

"Prayers that Protect and Transform"

Dr. Gregory Reed Frizzell

Powerful Prayer for Every Family *Prayers That Protect and Transform*
ISBN 978-1-941512-04-3
Copyright © 2008 Revised © 2014, All rights reserved by Gregory R. Frizzell.
Published by Master Design Publishing
      789 State Route 94 E., Fulton, KY 42041
      www.masterdesign.org

Printed by Bethany International in the USA

The Story of the Cover Artwork

The book photo features the prayer altar in the center part of our home. To us, it has very special meaning for two reasons. First, our Lord commands families to be centered on His presence. Without family prayer, no home can be fully centered upon Jesus. Second, the finely crafted walnut prayer altar was my wife's wedding gift to me. It was upon this altar that we took our vows in the church I pastored. To us, it symbolizes the covenant to keep our home centered on Jesus. With or without an actual prayer altar, any couple can make that commitment. Though no family is perfect, God will bless every home that seeks to put Him first. This book shows why no couple or single parent has to settle for anything less than dynamic prayer!

Conferences and Selected Resources by Dr. Gregory R. Frizzell

Key Conferences

Prayer That Transforms Loved Ones:
Winning The Spiritual War for Our Families

Going Deeper With God:
Journey to Personal and Church-wide Renewal

Selected Books

- How to Develop a Powerful Prayer Life *The Biblical Path to Holiness and Relationship with God*
- How to Pray without Ceasing
- Returning to Holiness *A Personal and Church-wide Journey to Revival* (Also available in Spanish translation)
- Return to Me Says the Lord *A Journey of First Love Surrender*
- Demolishing Personal and Church-wide Strongholds
- Biblical Patterns for Powerful Church Prayer Meetings *God's Changeless Path to Sweeping Revival and Evangelism*
- Releasing the Revival Flood *A Church-wide Journey to Miraculous Unity and God-Glorifying Fellowship*
- Saved, Certain and Transformed *Journey to Biblical Salvation, Full Assurance and Personal Revival*
- The Lord's Supper *A Covenant of Love and Surrender*
- Iceberg Dead Ahead *The Urgency of God-Seeking Repentance*

Resources by Dr. Gregory Frizzell may be ordered from:
Baptist General Convention of Oklahoma
3800 N. May Ave., Oklahoma City, OK 73112-6505
Phone: 405.990.3730 E-mail: gfrizzell@bgco.org
Or gfrizzell@earthlink.net or masterdesign.org

Table of Contents

Introduction

An Encouraging Word of Hope

As I write this tool, I've never felt more of God's compassion. Our merciful God is deeply touched by the battles and pressures of modern families. In a day when so many families are under attack, God's word provides another powerful pattern for protection and victory. That pattern is centering families around God and His Word. (Deuteronomy 6:6-10; Ephesians 5:25-6:4; 1 Peter 3:7) Beyond question, another most vital part of a Christ-centered home is marriage and family prayer!

Yet to many, this subject seems overwhelming or out of reach. No doubt, many feel a nagging sense of failure or are afraid it is just too late to start. For these concerns I have great news. Through God's grace, *any* family can find prayer patterns that work for them. Even parents with grown children or grandchildren can embrace effective prayer with remarkable results. This tool is designed to empower any parent or family at any stage in life.

Perhaps best of all, **Powerful Prayer for Every Family** is not some complicated, legalistic program we must all practice the same way. Rather, it is a flexible, God-focused tool to help all families pray with greater power. Because this book is simple, grace-based and Scripture-filled, there is no reason for any family to live in weakness or defeat.

The Urgency Has Never Been Greater!

While a major objective is to encourage parents about prayer, there is also a need for urgent warning. Because of severe and unprecedented spiritual attack on families, effective prayer is absolutely crucial. My purpose is to help every parent realize powerful prayer is not just important — it is *essential!* Current conditions have become so severe, parents must take this subject seriously or lose their children to the world's evil designs. Unfortunately, it is just about that simple.

The idea it is enough just to take kids to church is both unbiblical and dangerous. According to the Bible, *parents* must take the primary responsibility to pray for, protect and guide their children. While going to church is vitally important, it *cannot* replace consistent prayer and Bible teaching at home. To help their families, many pastors are giving this practical book to their congregations.

Again, let me assure every parent — by God's grace you *can* experience powerful prayer. Effective prayer is *not* out of reach! In Appendix C, I provide a specific covenant for prayer that protects and transforms our families. This book becomes your personal handbook and prayer journal for claiming promises. There is a Prayer and Promise Journal on page 52.

As you embrace your journey in deeper prayer, remember one great truth. God *will* bless and guide your efforts! His mercy, grace and power are greater than all your needs and failures. If you draw near to God, He will surely draw near to you! (James 4:8)

Toward Revived Families and God's Glory,

A Special Word to Pastors

In a day of unprecedented family devastation, something positive is occurring. A growing number of pastors are awakening to the extreme importance of preaching on powerful marriage and family prayer! More importantly, they are not only preaching on its importance, they are providing significant tools for practical help. Especially crucial is the need to teach modern families about "spiritual protection" and "united prayer for overcoming strongholds." They are teaching parents how to fight and win the spiritual war for their children!

Yet sadly, this trend of greater prayer emphasis is still only a small percentage of pastors. It was a great turning point in my own pastoral ministry when God helped me see my neglect of this most crucial area. Surely among our greatest failures is a neglect of practical teaching on family prayer and spiritual warfare for loved ones. While there is considerable material on marriage, the crucial area of "family prayer" is dangerously under-emphasized. Yet there is hope as many pastors are awakening to this most urgent need!

It is my deep desire to fan these flames by providing affordable resources with practical impact. For pastors, churches or individuals, we are able to provide **Powerful Prayer for Every Family** for incredibly low prices. Many pastors are providing them for all their families.

For further help, I offer a much expanded tool for pastors who want to preach a sermon (or teaching series) on marriage and family prayer. The tool **Essential Principles for Christ-centered Families,** is available to pastors in its pre-published version. It contains strong Scripture study and illustrations for preaching on marriage and families. I now also include a stronger family prayer element in my church and denominational conferences. For information on book orders or conferences, contact Dr. Frizzell at the address in the back of this book.

Chapter One
Foundational Patterns and Truths
"Prayers That Transform and Protect"

*T*hroughout the New Testament, we see the incredible power of united prayer. (Acts 1:14, 2:1, 4:29-31, 12:5-12) Surely there is no place prayer is more important than in the home. Studies clearly reveal the awesome difference between families that pray together and those that do not. "For couples that pray together every day, the divorce rate goes from a staggering one in two to just one in 1,052!" (Gallup Research Corporation) There is also an enormous difference in the lives of children whose parents pray with effectiveness.

With between seventy and eighty percent of children raised in church dropping out at age eighteen, we simply *must* embrace the kind of prayers and home Bible training that can change that trend. Beyond question, the Bible proclaims the extreme importance of homes being centered on God and His word. (Deuteronomy 6:6-10; Ephesians 5:25-6:4; 1 Peter 3:7)

Unfortunately, incredibly few Christian couples take this essential pattern seriously. It is further true that many who do pray, fail to pray effectively or specifically for their children and grandchildren. Most confess they have little knowledge of how to pray a "hedge of protection" around their marriage, children or grandchildren. It is little wonder so many marriages and children seem like "sitting ducks" for the enemy.

Powerful Family Prayer is Not Unreachable
Neither is it Too Late to Start!

In the face of modern pressures, many parents feel intimidated by the subject of family prayer. Still others feel that it's too late since their children are grown and they may even have grandchildren. Yet I have great news for every reader. *Powerful family prayer is not out of reach and it's not too late to start!* Even busy couples who have never prayed together can learn to experience awesome closeness with Jesus. Grandparents can learn to pray more effectively and see awesome changes in their families. It is amazing how often the Lord can still work in grown children and grandchildren. The vital thing is to reject discouragement and start *now!* We serve the God who can even restore years locusts have eaten away. (Joel 2:25)

There is no better way to begin than to describe three simple patterns for dynamic couples' prayer. First, I will describe two couples' prayer formats that are fairly brief and simple. The third pattern is more extensive but still not out of reach. At least periodically, couples should take time to go through something like pattern three. These outlines are drawn from **Powerful Marriage and Family Prayer** by Gregory Frizzell. Though they are brief, these patterns will help any couple pray together in power.

In this book, I also provide simple ways to take prayers for children to whole new levels of effectiveness. Yet, let me stress that none of these patterns are legalistic programs that couples must rigidly follow every day. Each couple will allow Jesus's unique guidance for their own frequency and patterns in prayer. How glorious to remember we are under grace not law! Though no couple will be perfect in their patterns, God will wonderfully bless their efforts to go deeper.

*(Couples should not feel they always have to follow these exact patterns or include every element. **Any** time couples spend in prayer is good time! While the following outline represents a healthy biblical pattern, it is not a rigid formula or law. Some couples may find it helpful to have a slightly abbreviated daily prayer time and experience this more extended time once a week.)*

Pattern One
Simple Morning or Evening Couple's Prayer Time

In this simple but powerful pattern, couples set aside a minimum of five to fifteen minutes for daily (or at least regular) prayer and sharing together. For spouses who have their individual quiet times in the morning, this requires getting up early enough to have their own devotion and then come together for their joint prayer time. For this reason, many couples may actually find it best to have their main couple's prayer time before they go to bed in the evening. With this pattern, they have their individual quiet times in the morning with perhaps just a brief joint prayer before leaving the home. Whenever possible, I believe it is good for couples to have at least some time to pray together before beginning their day.

Each pattern (morning or evening) has advantages and God will guide each couple in the approach best for them. Both patterns afford the opportunity for parents to specifically pray with children at a separate time. As I will address later, breakfast time and/or bed-time devotions are often good for praying with children. Morning or evening couples' prayer times generally do not interfere with either personal quiet times or prayer with children. These patterns are also easy to adjust as needed. Of course for couples with children, morning prayer would naturally have to be quite early.

As with all the patterns, I again stress they are merely guides, not rigid formulas. The main objective is allowing God's Spirit to guide in your devotion times. Some days He will lead you to significantly vary the order and content of your prayers. In other words, you are not bound to daily include all the elements in the suggestions for pattern two. Simply relax and trust God's direction. As you let Him guide, couples' prayer will become a natural, easy flowing relationship with God and each other. The results are phenomenal!

General Suggestion for Morning or Evening Prayers

✟ *Begin simply centering your hearts on God through heartfelt praise, thanksgiving and worship.* During these moments, allow God's Spirit to guide in praising Him for His grace, love and power. By so doing, you will enter a real sense of God's close presence. As you reflect on God's acceptance and grace in Christ, you are empowered to approach His throne with confidence. The more you sense the awesomeness and character of Who you're talking to, the more your prayers will be empowered. This cultivated awareness of God is a huge part of "hallowing His name."

✟ *An especially effective approach is to praise God using His many names revealed in Scripture (each name has a descriptive meaning.)* It is also powerful to praise Him using His characteristics (e.g. holy, loving, merciful, gracious, powerful, faithful, glorious, etc.) Reflecting on God's mighty acts deepens our confidence and faith. By praying in this manner, you hallow His name and center your heart on God's immediate presence. As you embrace the reality of His presence, your prayers become real and relational not rigid or legalistic.

✟ *Continue by sharing any insights you may have received from God's word or His activity in your life.* I strongly suggest either reading a portion of Scripture together or sharing insights from your individual quiet times or daily life. (John 10:27; James 1:5) It is an excellent time to share what God is doing or saying in your lives. Such sharing greatly increases a couple's closeness and growth. This alone will do much for the closeness of a marriage.

✟ *Ask God's cleansing, forgiveness and help for any sins or weaknesses you may be experiencing.* Claim His forgiveness in Jesus and resolve to embrace Christ's righteousness. (Proverbs 28:13; 1 John 1:9) Remember, there is no condemnation to those who are in Christ and walk by His Spirit. (Romans 8:1) Appropriately sharing weaknesses and struggles has enormous power for increasing intimacy and trust between couples.

✞ *Allow God to guide you in praying for a few key issues of eternal (kingdom or spiritual) significance.* Jesus tells us the main focus of our prayers is to be "His kingdom and His righteousness." Some good examples of kingdom prayer are: praying for revival, evangelism, missions, relationship healing, your church and its leaders, persecuted saints, etc. (Matthew 6:33)

✞ *Present to God what you perceive to be your important needs and desires.* It is important to present your requests with thanksgiving and faith in God's answers. Be sure to claim Scriptural promises for your needs. Above all, God wants us to trust Him even when answers are long delayed. Praying God's promises has very special power. (John 14:12-14; 2 Corinthians 1:20; Philippians 4:6-7)

✞ *A good way to end is simply praising God for His greatness and surrendering your lives to His Lordship. Also claim His guidance, provision and protection.* Especially today, praying for protection is vitally important. Leave your prayer time with the commitment to talk and listen to God throughout your day. Remember, you certainly don't leave God in your prayer closet. Prayer is by no means just for our quiet times! Talking and listening to God is a wonderful twenty-four hour lifestyle. (1 Thessalonians 5:17) The book, **How to Pray Without Ceasing** provides much practical helps for talking and listening to God all day.

Now that we have examined a fairly basic pattern for couples' prayer, we continue our journey by sharing two other patterns. The next pattern is very simple and the one following is more comprehensive. The best approach is to familiarize yourself with the various patterns and draw elements from each. Simply allow God to guide you to your own unique experience. One thing is certain — He will bless every sincere effort big or small.

Pattern Two
Spontaneous Conversational Couples' Prayer
"The Pattern with No Set Pattern"

This pattern is somewhat unique because with it, there really is no pattern. In this approach, couples simply focus their hearts on God and ask Him to guide in what and how they pray. I am especially fond of this approach because the primary desire is to seek "God's agenda" and give His Spirit complete control. It also lends itself to great freedom and spontaneity as couples pray whatever is on their heart. In this way, the pattern is very much a naturally flowing "conversation" with God and each other.

The conversational approach has enormous power for couples who may be unaccustomed to praying together. It can also be a good beginning place for young believers. One potential drawback is the fact some may get in a rut of praying in a narrow range of personal concerns. The more structured patterns are helpful toward insuring a biblical balance of focus.

Many couples actually combine elements from other patterns with the spontaneous approach. It is simple to do and the effect is awesome. Again, I suggest believers read through all the other patterns and highlight a few ideas that seem to best fit your needs and patterns. From the various patterns you can glean a few simple ideas that work for you. Don't make this hard or be uptight about formats. Concerning practical guidelines, I find three to be of particular help.

Guidelines for the Conversational Prayer Approach

(1) *As you begin your prayer time, sincerely ask God's leading and follow His quiet inner promptings.* After you have prayed about one issue, it is often good to pause and let God bring other matters to your minds. With this approach, couples often end up praying and hearing God on issues they had not even considered when they started. (That is a good sign you really are letting God guide.)

(2) *Try and avoid one spouse overly dominating the prayers.* This principle generally applies to all the patterns. It is often helpful to pray in briefer sentences and allow the prayers to be somewhat conversational. By conversational, I mean one prays a few sentences then gives the other opportunity to pick up the prayer. Of course, every couple is different and with some one party is much more comfortable praying aloud. In that case, the couple simply follows the flow that is most natural. One should not be pressured to pray much beyond their comfort level. (Although a little stretching helps us grow.)

(3) *It is often very helpful to pray in "subjects."* In other words, you may for a time target needs of family. During that time, each spouse will pray spontaneously for all that comes to mind regarding family. You would then move from subject to subject. Some common subjects are: salvation of lost people, healthy relationships, church and church leaders, revival, missions, certain people, family needs, direction, wisdom, protection, physical needs, praise and worship, etc.

As is obvious, the potential subjects for prayer are endless. The desired goal is letting Jesus guide you to various subjects. Each spouse then prays spontaneously as the Lord brings impressions regarding that area. (Of course, you would generally not pray through all the different ideas at one prayer time.)

However, I do recommend that couples guard against a rut of mostly self-focused prayers.

The beauty of this approach is its two-fold goal of (a) fully letting God lead and (b) the spontaneous and conversational manner in which it flows. It is also completely flexible in length and flow. In fact, I recommend the principle of God's guidance and conversational spontaneity for all the various patterns. These principles apply to virtually all the patterns.

Pattern Three
A More Expanded Couple's Prayer Time

(Pattern Three is similar to The Morning and Evening Prayer process. However, in Pattern Three couples generally go into greater depth and spend more time. God will guide couples in patterns best for them.)

1. After reading a section of God's word, spend a few moments thanking and praising God together. Focus on the greatness, love and power of holy God. Reflect on the fact Christ's blood and grace makes you wholly acceptable in His sight. (*Some couples may choose to read God's Word *after* their praise time.) Take a moment to discuss any directions or insights you received from God's Word.

2. Spend a few minutes asking God's forgiveness for specific sins. (Of course you will use discretion and wisdom in what you share with one another.) Pray for God's strength in areas of weakness.

3. Pray for kingdom issues such as: salvation of the lost, blessing on your marriage, strengthening your church, revival, persecuted believers and God's guidance for leaders. It is especially important to pray for lost people, missions and for spiritual awakening. Ask God for spiritual protection and deliverance from Satan schemes. Ask the Lord to tear down any strongholds in your lives,

family or church. Be specific in targeting strongholds. In your praying, always seek to focus more on character and spiritual growth than mere temporal concerns.

4. Bring your key needs and desires to God in prayer. Always pray for direction, spiritual empowerment and protection.

5. Briefly discuss any impressions or insights you sense from God. End with praise to God and surrender of your lives to Christ's Lordship. Under the next heading I provide practical descriptions of how to embrace this more expanded prayer pattern.

An Expanded Explanation of Powerful Couples' Prayer

1. Spend a Few Minutes in Praise, Thanksgiving, Worship and Scripture

After a daily Bible reading together, let each briefly share what the passages said to them. If you are not doing a Bible reading together, simply begin with a time of praising and thanking God. (Psalms 100:4-5) I suggest you hallow God's name by praising Him for some of His characteristics (i.e. love, mercy, power, grace, faithfulness, patience, holiness, glory, truth, kindness, etc.) You could then thank God for past, present and future blessings (i.e. salvation, physical blessings, finances, guidance, strength, provision, healing, etc.) Be sensitive to let His Spirit guide in genuine praise, not rote repetition.

2. Embrace a Time of Repentance, Confession and Yielding to Christ's Lordship

Ask God's forgiveness for sins and ask one another for forgiveness (if there is a need). Claim God's wonderful promise of grace.

(1 John 1:9) Pray for one another in areas that need growth. Do not stop with confession – make sure you are moving to genuine repentance. (Proverbs 28:13) Periodically, each spouse should (separately) pray through a thorough cleansing guide to ensure they are praying in the power of God's Spirit. (Psalms 24:3, 66:18, 139:23-24; James 5:15) It is vital to understand that unconfessed sin and unyielded hearts enormously hinder the power of our prayers. (*Use the cleansing guide listed on page 37 of this tool.*)

3. *Spend a Few Moments Interceding for Kingdom Issues (Intercession and Spiritual Warfare)*

Pray for spiritual needs such as: salvation of lost people, spiritual growth of spouse, children, family or others. During this time, you could ask God to tear down any strongholds or deliver from specific attacks that are underway. (Matthew 6:13) You may also want to pray for your pastor, church, missions, revival and special leaders. Pray for your preacher and key leaders to heed God's guidance. Pray for God's mercy upon our nation and world.

4. *Lift Your Personal and Family Needs to the Father (Supplication/Petition)*

Pray for the earthly needs and concerns of yourself and others. (Philippians 4:6-7) These may be concerns for physical health, relational concerns or financial needs. During this time you would also pray for guidance and protection. A powerful guideline for your petitions is to seek to focus more on the development of spiritual character than on early needs alone. The Fruits of the Spirit and Beatitudes are excellent guides for personal and/or family petitions. In praying for spouses and children, I urge you to be more specific and biblical than vague and general. (The material in the next chapters provides much guidance for effective, Scripture-based prayer.)

5. Meditation on God's Word and Insights (Listening to God's Voice)

Share any insights or impressions from your time in Scripture and prayer. It is important to begin to see prayer as a dialogue of both talking *and* listening to God. (Psalm 1:2, Isaiah 55:3) True prayer is not just a ritual of presenting prayers, it is listening for the Lord's impressions, promises and insights. It is a living relationship with the living Christ. End with praise and thanksgiving to God. Surrender yourselves to Christ's Lordship and trust Him to guide your steps.

How to Embrace Powerful "Biblical" Prayers
"What We Pray Truly Matters!"

Now that we have examined three basic biblical patterns for regular or periodic couple's prayer, we turn our attention to specific prayer guides that are biblical and powerful. Make no mistake it really does matter *how* and *what* we pray! It is the *"effective, fervent prayer of the righteous that avail much."* (James 5:16b) If how we pray didn't matter, God would not have listed so many specific, insightful prayers in Scripture.

In this book, I outline biblical prayers that are effective and specific. But again, you should view these as helpful guides not "magic prayers" or legalistic requirements. Yet, letting God's Spirit guide in biblical prayers helps insure your prayers are in His will. When we pray God's will in the power of His Spirit, the results are awesome. If we *"ask according to His will, we know He hears us!"* (1 John 5:14-15)

Over the next few pages, I provide three sets of biblical prayers for our families as well as ourselves. We also present practical tools for spiritual cleansing and miraculous spiritual breakthrough. The strategy for breakthrough is called the "united prayer blitz."

Lest anyone feel overwhelmed, let me stress the various tools are "options" from which each reader chooses. No one should feel obligated to use all of the various prayers and tools all the time. Simply select a few key points and apply them as God leads. For clarity, it will help readers to briefly overview the contents of the coming sections. In this book, we examine five practical tools for family prayer and spiritual breakthrough.

Five Powerful Prayer Tools
"Practical Options for Every Family

First, we will learn biblical prayers for praying a hedge of blessing and protection. As never before, it is vital to know how to effectively pray protection for ourselves and our loved ones.

Second, we provide a thirty day guide especially targeting our children. Each prayer is totally flexible for use by any family.

Third, we present a "Seven Category Method" for effective family prayers. While these are not rigid prayers to repeat verbatim, they do provide simple patterns to guide believers into effective, Spirit-empowered prayer.

Fourth, we provide a spiritual cleansing guide that is powerful for individuals or couples. The cleansing process is simple yet very thorough. Spiritual cleansing revolutionizes our sense of joy and our power in prayer.

Fifth, we explain the "united prayer blitz" or "praying in one accord" for spiritual breakthrough. This simple strategy utilizes the biblical principle of united agreement for powerful victory and answered prayer.

When reading the various prayer patterns, please feel free to use them interchangeably. Many people mix points from the different patterns to create their own unique process. While the prayer guides are powerful as presented, be sensitive to ways God may lead you to incorporate patterns unique to you. The guides consist of prayers for protection and thirty Scripture-based prayers that cover virtually every area of life and relationship with God. In this book, the practical prayer guides are listed as "Options One, Two and Three." Above all, let this book become a personal handbook and prayer journal for loved ones.

Create Your Own Prayer Journal and Promise Book
A Tool for Protecting and Transforming Loved Ones

This resource is not intended as a book you read and lay aside. I urge readers to use the book with a highlighter pen in hand. In each of the prayer options, believers will sense that certain prayers have unique significance for their children or spouse. I encourage readers to highlight that prayer and put it as a promise to claim in your prayer journal. (see page 52)

In the back of the book, I provide a page entitled **Key Prayers and Promises for Loved Ones**. On that page, I suggest recording key prayers and promises you are claiming for certain people. A journal of promises provide both a reminder and a record of God's direction. This tool is a powerful way to keep your prayers focused and a record of glorious testimonies when God answers!

Chapter Two

Powerful Prayers that Protect and Transform

Option One
"Praying a Spiritual Hedge of Protection"

*T*he concept of a "spiritual hedge" is derived from Job 1:10 and several passages in the Psalms that speak of God's protection. While it is often thought of as a hedge of protection, it can also mean a hedge of blessing and protection (as was implied in Job.) Because God has chosen to work powerfully through prayer, it is vital that parents and spouses pray effective prayers for those in their sphere of responsibility.

Even in the Lord's Prayer, Jesus directly mentioned the phrase "deliver us from evil." (Matthew 6:13) The Greek word for deliver (*rhuomai*) carries the idea of being delivered, saved (and protected) from sin, temptation, Satan and physical or spiritual harm. Believers should remember that prayer for protection and deliverance is just as much a part of the model prayer as "forgive us our trespasses." Remember also that the model prayer is a direct command and instruction — Jesus said, *"Pray in this manner."* (Matthew 6:9)

In the disciple's prayer of John 17:11 and 15, Jesus twice prayed that believers be "kept" from the evil one. In this text, the Greek word for kept (*te'reo'*) means guarding, preserving or protecting. Since Jesus Himself specifically commanded and *practiced* the element of protection in His two most foundational prayers, why would we think we can ignore it? We do so at great risk.

As with other elements of prayer, it is important that we pray for protection with biblical effectiveness. A crucial part of spiritual protection is the principle of both "putting off" evil and "putting on" Christ. (Romans 12:17-21; Colossians 3:8-10) In other words, you not only need to claim your loved ones' deliverance *from* evil but also their filling *with* Christ's life and righteousness. Our goal in praying is not just for "protection," but also for progressive "transformation." Mark this well — our best protection from evil is to be filled with the righteousness of Christ. God mostly delivers us from evil, by replacing it with Christ's righteousness in us. (Galatians 2:20; Colossians 1:27)

Protecting and Transforming Our Essential Areas
Understanding the "Spiritual Gates" of a Person's Life

While there are some good books and suggestions for praying a hedge of protection, I believe seven basic areas should be a central focus in any approach. In essence, there are seven key areas or "spiritual gates" to the life of every person. When sin, bondage or deception enters a life, it comes through one or more) of seven entry points.

Understanding the key life areas helps us pray for loved ones specifically and thoroughly. The following areas are key to the protection and transformation of anyone's life: (1) *Heart* (spirit), (2) *Mind* (thoughts, motives and will), (3) *Affections* (desires and emotions), (4) *Relationships* (with God, self and others), (5) *Eyes and ears* (what we see and hear), (6) *Physical and financial*, (7) *Satanic attack, deception and oppression*.

Though we certainly do not necessarily have to pray for all areas each day, we should at least be aware of the seven primary gates to a person's life. It is important that we learn to pray with reasonable biblical depth and thoroughness. As believers become aware of the seven areas for protection and transformation, God's Spirit can more easily prompt their praying with insight.

When believers establish the habit of insightful praying over the key areas of a person's life, the process soon becomes second nature. Their prayers take on far greater focus, specificity and discernment. Intercessors will develop a Spirit-guided sensitivity to know when to pray over certain areas more than others.

Again, do not let this process be complicated or legalistic. As we become familiar with the basic areas for protection, God will naturally bring them to mind as needed. When we learn to let God guide us in this type of prayer, the impact is profound and lasting. Before I present the **Seven Prayers for Protection and Transformation**, it will help to cover a few foundational truths about believers' growth, power and victory through prayer.

The Principle of Positive, Faith-Filled Prayer Focus
"Putting Off Evil – Putting On Christ"

As well as simply praying for "protection," it is vital to pray also for their "transformation" with righteousness. In other words, when you pray for someone to be protected from evil thoughts, pray also that they be filled with righteous thoughts. Again, we are delivered and protected from evil by "replacing" it with good. Believers, we must not focus merely on "getting rid of evil" but on "embracing righteousness." God is not interested in simply helping us (or those we pray for) avoid evil. He wants to transform us into the image of Christ. (Romans 8:1-29)

Beyond question, confession alone is not enough. God desires confession, cleansing *and* repentance. (Proverbs 28:13; 1 John 1:9) A prime example is found in Jesus' statement in Matthew 12:43-45. In these passages, our Lord describes the reality of a demon being cast out only to return to the person bringing seven other spirits even more wicked. If it finds the person empty (and vulnerable) the evil returns many times worse.

Jesus' words in Matthew reveal the importance of praying to be filled with Christ's righteousness as well as being delivered from evil. In essence, spiritual fullness is our most powerful protection. Yet concerning these points, there is great news for every reader. None of this is done in our own strength — it is in learning to let Christ flow through us by faith. (Romans 6:11-14; Colossians 1:27)

In our day of shallow prayer, it has never been more important to embrace practical patterns for greater depth. It is also important to pray in a balanced, biblical and effective manner. When we pray with even a little more depth and power, the difference is enormous. But again, don't be discouraged or think any of this is difficult! The two elements of effective prayer are really quite simple. Prayerfully consider the following two elements of powerful prayer.

A first element is having a God-focused goal and kingdom purpose. A God-focused goal means your first priority is seeking Jesus will and Lordship in your life (and others). In other words, your central motive is not just getting blessed. It is to be transformed to hallow and glorify God's Name. As we truly learn to "seek first His kingdom and righteousness," protection and blessing are automatic. (Matthew 6:33) Best of all, it is Christ's grace and strength flowing through us!

In many ways there is great truth to the old adage — *the best defense is a good offense!* If a person's life is not filled with God's Spirit and righteousness, he or she is an easy mark for the devil. (Matthew 12:43-45) Yet as we keep our eyes on Jesus, we are changed into His image and filled with all righteousness. (2 Corinthians 3:18; Hebrews 12:2) Remember again the vital principle — God mostly delivers us from evil by replacing it with righteousness. "*Do not be overcome of evil, but overcome evil with good.*" (Romans 12:21)

In the next section, I provide sample prayers that follow the "put off – put on" pattern of positive focus. As you will notice, the prayers are fairly simple. Soon this type of prayer becomes very natural and spontaneous in our lives.

A second element of effective prayer is Spirit-empowered, expectant faith. When we pray for things we know are God's will, we can and should pray in faith. God's word makes very clear the importance of praying in faith. (Mark 11:22-24); James 1:5-7; 1 John 5:14-15) One thing is certain — when you pray for protection from sin and filling with righteousness, you are praying in God's will.

All of the prayer guides in this book follow the biblical patterns of faith and positive focus. By following this pattern, we avoid an over-focus on sin while keeping our eyes on Jesus. It is important and liberating to learn to keep our eyes on Jesus, *not* our own sin and weakness. Let God guide you in the prayers, wording and frequency that is right for you.

Seven Prayers for Protection and Transformation
"Delivered from Evil – Filled with the Spirit"

1. **Protecting and Transforming the Heart** — Father, I trust you to guard (insert names) their hearts and help them ever look to You in love and reverence. By Your grace, cause them to know, love and fear Your name. Guard their hearts from all lesser desires and passions. Lord, please fill them with the continual sense of Your presence and spirit of worship. (Proverbs 4:23; Matthew 15:8, 22:37; John 4:23-24, 17:3)

2. **Protecting and Transforming the Mind** — Lord Jesus, I believe You to guard (insert names) minds and cause their thoughts to be taken captive to Yourself. Protect them from the suggestions of the world, the flesh and the devil. Fill them with the Holy Spirit and the very mind and thoughts of Christ. (2 Corinthians 10:5; 1 Corinthians 2:16)

3. **Protecting and Transforming Desires, Emotions and Passions** — Dear Lord, I trust You to guard (insert names) desires, emotions and passions. Protect and shield them from improper attractions. Please fill them with hunger and thirst for righteousness. Grant them a passion to glorify

and hallow Your name. Deliver them from the works of the flesh and fill them with the fruit of the Spirit. (Matthew 5:6; Galatians 5:18-22)

4. **Protecting and Transforming Relationships** — Holy Father, I believe You to guard (insert names) from harmful relationships. Surround them with godly companions, friends and co-workers. Grant powerful awareness and strong conviction when a relationship is becoming unwholesome or wrong. Protect them from wrong involvements and fill them with supernatural wisdom. (2 Corinthians 6:14)

5. **Protecting and Transforming the Eyes and Ears** — Blessed Lord, I trust You to guard (insert names) eyes and ears from evil and fill their minds with Christ. Grant keen discernment when they see or hear evil. When they see or hear evil, cause their hearts to be repulsed, not enticed. Fill them with pure eyes, a clean mind and deep conviction of truth. (Proverbs 4:23; Matthew 6:22)

6. **Protecting and Transforming Areas of Physical, Financial and Spiritual Risk** — Sovereign Lord, I believe You to guard (insert names) physically, spiritually, emotionally, mentally and financially. Please send mighty angels to hedge their paths and protect their steps. Fill them with blessing, health, safety, guidance and purpose. Cause them to clearly hear Your voice and walk in Your steps. Bless them indeed and use them for Your glory. (1 Chronicles 4:9-10; Psalm 23, 91; 3 John 2)

7. **Protecting and Transforming Areas of Satanic Attack, Deception and Harassment** —Blessed Savior, I trust You to guard (insert names) from all attack, deception, harassment and harm from Satan and his demons. Open their eyes to the deceptions and tactics of the Devil. Fill their minds with Your

truth. Please tear down any strongholds or vulnerabilities in their lives. (Name any stronghold and tear them down by the weapons of prayer and Scripture.) (2 Corinthians 10:3-5; Ephesians 6:10) Lord, cause Satan to release his grip and flee from their lives. Put about them the whole armor of truth, righteousness, peace and the shield of faith. *For their particular stronghold or weakness, pray for them to be filled with the opposite trait of spiritual strength (i.e. fear/peace, anger/gentleness, lust/purity, wrong desires/right desires, pride/humility, etc.)

Include Periodic Prayer for Key Leaders
(1 Timothy 2:1-2)

Though this book is mostly about praying for spouses and children, I also urge consistent prayer for your spiritual leaders. We are living in a time when pastors and their families are failing at unprecedented rates. In addition to widespread moral failures, pornography is exploding in all age groups.

Tragically, failure has also exploded among clergy. If ever there was a time to be praying a "hedge of protection' around our families and spiritual leaders that time is now! As you pray for your family, *I encourage all families to include at least a brief prayer for their pastors and key leaders.* This is a biblical habit God will surely bless.

Whatever you do, please do not take this issue lightly. God's name has been profaned and His gospel hindered by scandalous public failures in spiritual leaders. If we do not faithfully intercede for our families, pastors and spiritual leaders, we can expect even more devastating failures. The world, flesh and devil have mounted an all-out attack. We must meet these attacks with effective, warfare praying.

Pray for Spiritual Awakening

I also urge every believer to pray for revival and spiritual awakening. The conditions of our nation are now so severe, a sweeping spiritual awakening is our only hope for major change. Indeed, your children's future will be greatly impacted by whether or not we have revival. Yet if millions of believers pray for the nation, God could still touch our land.

For practical help in praying for revival, see **Appendix A** in the back of the book. It is also important to pray for the lost and teach our children to do the same. **Appendix B** provides simple but powerful help in praying for the lost. **Appendix C** is a specific biblical covenant to solidify parents' commitment to pray effectively for their children and spouse.

Option Two

Biblical Prayers Specifically for Children
Powerful Prayers to Pray

Special note to parents or grandparents: Do not be overwhelmed by the list of thirty biblical prayers for children. I am *not* suggesting you have to pray all these each time you pray! One option is to pray one each day. With that pattern, you would get through all each month. Another pattern is to pray three points a day. In that flow you would pray through all thirty biblical prayers three times each month.

Another strong option is to simply mark a few prayers that are especially urgent for your children at this time. By so doing, this tool becomes a working handbook for continual use. As you let God guide, your prayers become much more specific and thus more powerful.

Beyond question, our children deserve powerful specific prayer, not vague generalities. To fail our children by inconsistent, shallow prayer is among the greatest of all failures. To fail to pray effectively for our children is to leave them dangerously vulnerable and lacking in spiritual power. When combined with prayers for protection, the following biblical prayers are very powerful.

1. That God would draw them to Himself at an early age (John 3:3, 6:44)

2. That they love the Lord their God with all their heart (Matthew 22:37-39)

3. That they love others as they love themselves (Matthew 22:37-39)

4. That they know and love God's Word (Psalm 119:9-11)

5. That they would love Christ's Church (Ephesians 4:14-16)

6. That they be protected from the deceits and schemes of Satan (Ephesians 6:11)

7. For their moral purity (Proverbs 5:7-23; 1 Thessalonians 4:3)

8. For them to obey and respect authority (Exodus 20:12)

9. For them to be wise in the wisdom of the Lord (Proverbs 1:7)

10. That they would understand the reason for persecution and endure hardship in joyful fellowship with Christ (Colossians 1:24; 2 Timothy 3:12)

11. That their *yes* would be a yes and their *no* would mean no and have strong integrity (Matthew 5:37)

12. That they be equally yoked to a godly spouse (2 Corinthians 6:14) Pray for their future mates now.

13. That they would be always humble, desiring for God to have the glory (2 Timothy 4:18)

14. That their life would be used to promote God's kingdom (Matthew 28:18-20)

15. That they would understand grace and so live out the law of Christ by His Spirit (Titus 2:11)

16. That they hunger and thirst for God's righteousness (Matthew 5:6)

17. That they hate evil, avoid it and be convicted when they disobey (Proverbs 4:14)

18. That they would think biblically and immediately spot spiritual error (2 Corinthians 10:5; Romans 12:1-2)

19. That they be secure in who God has made them to be (Romans 8:1; Ephesians 1:6)

20. For them to be salt and light (Matthew 5:13-16)

21. That they know they are deeply loved (Psalm 103)

22. For them to be hard workers (Colossians 1:28-20)

23. For them to be an encourager to others (Hebrews 10:24)

24. That they would have honesty with the Lord, themselves and others (1 John 1:1-9)

25. That they be faithful stewards of their God-given talents (1 Timothy 6:6-10)

26. That they live by an eternal perspective (Philippians 3:20)

27. That my girl(s) would have a quiet and gentle spirit and my boy(s) would be the spiritual leader of his family (1 Peter 3:4; Ephesians 5:23)

28. For them to identify with femaleness/maleness and be protected from gender confusion (Romans 1:25-28)

29. That they would have and be a special friend (David and Jonathan – 1 Samuel 20)

30. That they would glorify God in whatever health or life circumstances He gives them, rejoicing always (1 Thessalonians 5:18)

Option Three

"The Seven Category Method"
Praying for Children and Others
by Essential Categories

An especially powerful pattern is the seven category prayer method. The power of this approach is in its simplicity and thoroughness. It is also powerful because it covers all seven essential areas of a person's life. This approach is as powerful in praying for yourself as for your children and spouse.

As with the other approaches, it is used as a Spirit-guided tool, not a ritualistic requirement. It is equally powerful for both intercession or personal petition. These seven categories are incredibly powerful in praying for yourself.

I encourage readers to read the seven categories and choose a *few* key requests from each one. In all likelihood, you will only pray for a few each day. However, it is incredibly powerful to at least periodically pray through all the issues.

Some couples (or single parents) set aside significant time once every few weeks to pray through all seven areas. By so doing, you pray for your children in a more powerful and thorough manner. As with the other patterns, let God guide in the approach that is right for you. With God's guidance, the seven category method takes your prayers to a whole new level.

Category One — Praying For Their Relationship with God

1. That (insert names) will walk in intense love for God and reverential fear of His holy name. Also pray that they love their neighbor as themselves. (Proverbs 1:7; Ecclesiastes 12:13; Matthew 22:37-39)

2. That (insert names) would seek first the kingdom of God and His righteousness in all things at all times. (Matthew 6:33) Pray that they would have a passion for soul-winning and missions. (Acts 1:8)

3. That (insert names) would have a passion to hallow and glorify God's name in all places at all times. (Matthew 6:9)

4. That (insert names) will know how long, wide, deep and high is the love of Christ and to know the love that surpasses knowledge. (Ephesians 3:17-19)

5. That (insert names) will be mightily filled with the Holy Spirit and take every thought captive to Jesus. (Luke 11:13; Ephesians 5:18; 2 Corinthians 10:5)

6. That (insert names) will allow God to work in his/her life to accomplish His purposes for him/her. (Philippians 2:12-13)

7. That (insert names) will be filled with a spirit of prayer and hunger for God's Word and Presence. (Psalm 42:1; John 15:7; 1 Thessalonians 5:17)

8. That (insert names) will seek and receive wisdom with understanding. (Proverbs 2:1-5; Ephesians 1:17-18)

9. That (insert names) will earnestly seek God and love Christ's Church. (Psalm 63:1, 122:1)

10. That (insert names) will be deeply convicted of sin and have godly sorrow that brings repentance. (Psalm 119:71; 2 Corinthians 7:10)

11. That (insert names) will submit to God, resist the devil and be surrounded by a powerful hedge of spiritual protection. (James 4:7)

12. That (insert names) will intimately know God, clearly hear His voice and discern truth. (John 10:27, 17:3)

13. That (insert names) will daily die to themselves and embrace the cross and be willing to suffer for His name sake. . (1 Corinthians 15:21; Luke 14:27)

14. That (insert names) will be filled with the burning desire and power to know God and do His will. (Philippians 2:13)

Category Two — Praying For Godly Attributes and Holy Character

1. That they will display the nine fruits of the Spirit; love, joy, peace, patience, kindness, goodness, faithfulness, gentleness and self-control. (Galatians 5:22-23)

2. That they will manifest the beatitudes in daily life. (Poor in spirit, mourning, meek, hunger and thirst for righteousness, merciful, pure in heart, peacemakers, persecuted for righteousness. (Matthew 5:1-12)

3. That they will deeply fear and reverence God being continually aware of His Presence. (Psalm 139:7-12; Ecclesiastes 12:13; Matthew 6:9)

4. That they will be strengthened in the inner person and continually filled with the Holy Spirit. (Ephesians 3:16-17)

5. That they will hate sin. (Psalm 97:10)

6. That they will respect authority. (Romans 13:1)

7. That they be protected from attitudes of personal inferiority or superiority. (Genesis 1:27; Philippians 2:3)

8. That they will be able to control anger. (Ephesians 4:26)

9. That they will be able to endure hardships and trials with patience and strength. (Matthew 5:12; 2 Timothy 2:3)

10. That they will suffer attack and persecution with grace and rejoicing. (Matthew 5:12; James 1:2)

Category Three — Praying For Family Relationships

1. That children will honor and obey their parents in the Lord. (Proverbs 1:8; Colossians 3:20)

2. That children will accept discipline and profit from it. (Proverbs 3:11-12, 23:19)

3. That each child will love his/her siblings and not allow rivalry to hinder their having a lifelong positive relationship. (Matthew 5:22)

4. That as parents we may so live before them to entice him/her to God's kingdom, not drive him/her away. (Matthew 5:16)

5. That the husband will sacrificially love his wife as Christ loved the Church, treasuring her and dwelling with her in kind understanding. (Ephesians 5:25; 1 Peter 3:7)

6. That the husband will be the spiritual head of the home, training and bringing up children in the nurture and admonition of the Lord. (Ephesians 5:27, 6:2-4)

7. That no family bitterness or division will be allowed to remain unconfessed and un-surrendered. (Matthew 5:23; 6:14-15; Ephesians 4:26)

8. That the wife will reverence her husband and love her family with a sacrificial love. (Proverbs 31:10-20) Pray for her to meet their emotional, physical and spiritual needs.

Category Four — Praying For Their Relationships with Fellow Believers, Friends and Peers

1. That they will embrace loving, koinonia relationships with fellow believers. (John 13:34-35, 17:21; Acts 2:42-47, 4:32-33)

2. That they will be a humble servant to all and reject any form of self exaltation or self promotion. (Matthew 23:11-12)

3. That they will choose godly friends who will build him/her up in the Lord. (Proverbs 27:9; Ecclesiastes 4:10)

4. That they will desire the right kind of friends and he/she will be kept from harmful friendships that may lead him/her astray. (Proverbs 1:10)

5. That they will be firm in his/her convictions and be able to withstand peer pressure. (Ephesians 4:14)

6. That they will befriend the lonely, the discouraged and the lost. (Matthew 25:40; Philippians 2:4)

7. That they will pro-actively serve and do good for fellow believers, friends and enemies. (Matthew 5:43-48)

8. That they will embrace God's grace to do good to those who persecute them. (Matthew 5:12)

9. Pray they will contribute to the bond of peace, love and unity in their church and family. (John 13:34-35; Ephesians 4:3-4)

10. Pray that they will be peacemakers and contribute to a positive loving atmosphere with friends, family and church. (Matthew 5:9; Philippians 4:8)

11. That they be ever mindful of their example, testimony and witness to all they encounter. (Acts 1:8)

12. That God will prepare your children for their future mates and their mates for them. Pray that God will protect and preserve them one for another. (Romans 8:28)

Category Five — Praying For Their Ministry, Spiritual Gifts and Kingdom Service

1. That they will discern their spiritual gifts and have a passion for kingdom ministry and service to God. (1 Corinthians 12)

2. That they will have a burning passion for evangelism, discipleship, soul-winning and missions. (Matthew 28:18-20)

3. That they will discern God's personal vision for their life and ministry. (Proverbs 29:18; Jeremiah 29:11)

4. That God will use them as a vessel of honor in service for His Kingdom. (2 Timothy 2:21)

5. That they will abound in the work of the Lord and bear much fruit that remains. (1 Corinthians 15:58; John 15:16)

6. That they will be immovable and steadfast in spiritual growth and in serving God. (1 Corinthians 15:58)

7. That they will be filled with the heart of a servant to God and others. (Matthew 20:26)

8. That they will minister and serve with selfless purity of motive and unfeigned humility. (1 Peter 5:5; James 4:1-4)

9. That they will be filled with a willingness to sacrifice for Christ and His Kingdom. (Luke 14:26-33)

10. That they will count it an honor to suffer for Jesus. (Acts 5:41; Philippians 1:29)

Category Six — Praying For Deliverance and Protection

1. That they are protected from Satan in each area of his/her life – physically, mentally, emotionally, relationally and spiritually. (Matthew 6:13; John 17:15)

2. That they are protected from drugs, alcohol and tobacco. (Proverbs 20:18-23)

3. That they are protected from overwhelming fleshly desires. (Romans 6:6-14)

4. That they immediately recognize the deceits and schemes of the devil. (Ephesians 6:10-13)

5. That they are protected from the love of the world, lusts of the flesh and pride of life. (1 John 2:15-16)

6. That they are protected from the evil influence of the Internet, Hollywood and the music industry. (Psalm 1:1-3; Proverbs 1:10-11)

7. That they are protected from the influence of anti-God curriculum, teachers and godless professors seeking to indoctrinate with their narrow bias. (2 Corinthians 10:5)

8. That evil philosophies and teachings will find no root in their hearts. Pray for their minds and hearts to be filled with wisdom, discernment and truth. (2 Corinthians 10:5; Romans 12:1-2)

9. That God would send angels to surround and bear them up lest they fall. (Psalm 91:11-12)

10. That God would shelter them under the shadow of His wing. (Psalm 91:1-3)

Category Seven — Praying For Their Blessing, Comfort and Health

1. That God will bless them indeed and enlarge the territory of their coasts. (1 Chronicles 4:9-10 — *Prayer of Jabez*)

2. That God would surround their life with overwhelming mercy, grace and favor. (Psalm 91:1-16)

3. That they will prosper in all things and be in good health. (3 John verse 2)

4. That goodness and mercy will follow them all the days of their life. (Psalm 23:6)

5. That they will have renewed strength to run and not be weary, to walk and not faint. (Isaiah 40:31)

6. That God will daily restore their soul and lead them in abundant provision and peace that passes understanding. (Psalm 23:1-3; Philippians 4:7)

7. That the joy of the Lord will be their strength. (Philippians 4:13)

8. That God will comfort them in all their afflictions. (2 Thessalonians 2:17)

9. That God will do exceeding abundantly above all they ask or even think. (Ephesians 3:20)

10. That they continually experience abundant life and rivers of living water flowing from their inner-most being. (John 7:38, 10:10)

11. That God will be the love of their life and that they walk daily filled with all the fullness of Christ. (Matthew 22:37; Ephesians 1:23)

12. That they will walk in great favor with God and people. (Psalm 30:5; Acts 2:47)

Now that we have examined three different patterns of biblical prayers, every individual and couple has the tools for mountain-moving intercession. To complete the journey to spiritual victory, two more practical principles will have phenomenal impact.

In Chapter Three, we examine two life-changing principles: (1) Thorough spiritual cleansing for fullness and power as well as (2) the power of united prayer and fasting with specific focus. (The united prayer blitz) When these become a part of individual or family prayer, results are truly miraculous.

Chapter Three

Two Steps for Cleansing and Spiritual Breakthrough

*N*ow that readers are equipped with quality options for dynamic biblical prayers, two additional steps bring even greater power. Unfortunately, many modern believers have prayed without seeing their needed breakthroughs. A major reason is the intensified spiritual warfare that characterizes today's world. Though attack has accelerated dramatically, most believers are still praying on fairly low levels.

In the following section, I describe two vital biblical steps for intensified power. Though these two principles are simple and life-changing, it is astounding how few believers understand them. For readers who embrace these biblical steps, life will never be the same. Prayerfully consider adding two steps to your experience with God.

Step One for Greater Power and Breakthrough
"Embrace Periodic Times of Spiritual Cleansing"

According to God's Word, unconfessed sin is a *huge* hindrance to power in prayer. Full submission to God is crucial for resisting and overcoming Satan's attacks. (James 4:6; Psalm 66:18) It is further true that the cleansing of our hearts must be deep and thorough in order to be effective. (Psalm 139:23-24) The two principles are: (1) full spiritual cleansing and (2) united prayer for spiritual breakthrough in ourselves or loved one. Yet today, many believers either omit ongoing cleansing or rush through it in a brief and shallow manner. As a result, they experience little power and many prayers go unanswered. It is wonderful to be able to report that God has a perfect solution!

To experience deep cleansing, fullness and power in prayer, two suggestions will prove invaluable. *First*, periodically take time to pray through the cleansing guide (provided below).

Second, make effective cleansing a consistent part of your own prayer life. Though you certainly don't have to work through the entire cleansing guide each time you pray, at least some significant cleansing should nearly always be a part. Keeping a very short sin account is *crucial* to staying close to full intimacy and power with Christ. The following cleansing guide is designed for personal prayer and confession or church-wide use. Make no mistake — thorough cleansing will make a *huge* difference in the power of your prayers! (Psalms 66:18)

A Cleansing Guide for Fullness and Power
A Guide for Personal Confession and Repentance

If our prayers and witness are to have life-changing power, God's saints must be deeply yielded and filled with God's Spirit. (Psalm 66:18; Acts 1:8) To draw near to God, I urge every believer and church to embrace the following journey of cleansing and empowerment. (James 4:8) Yet as we embrace times of cleansing, let us remember three key truths.

(1) We are fully accepted in Christ's blood and righteousness. Let us keep our eyes on God's grace and not be defeated by condemnation. God convicts to transform, not condemn His children. (2) Do not just confess sins, work also on forsaking them! (Proverbs 28:13) (3) Believe Christ to live through you. Daily ask Jesus to fill you with His powerful presence. As you incorporate deeper cleansing, you can now trust God to empower your heart for effective prayer and witness.

Seven Areas for Cleansing and Victory

1. **Pure Thoughts** — *"For as he thinks in his heart, so is he."* (Proverbs 23:7a) *"Casting down arguments and every high thing that exalts itself against the knowledge of God, bringing every thought into captivity to the obedience of Christ."* (2 Corinthians 10:5)

   Fully confess and forsake whatever sins God brings to mind. Trust God to fill and empower you with His Spirit. After each of the following questions, pause and allow God to speak. (a) Do I have any pattern of unclean or lustful thoughts? ___ (b) Do I think far more about worldly things than spiritual? ___ (c) Am I often guilty of angry thoughts? ___ (d) Do I frequently entertain thoughts of doubt instead of trust? ___ (e) Am I often filled with thoughts of bitterness and unforgiveness? Believe Christ to live through you by the Holy Spirit. (Romans 6:11) Put off sinful thoughts and put on Christ by faith.

2. **Godly Attitudes** — *"Let this mind (attitude) be in you, which was also in Christ Jesus."* (Philippians 2:5)

   Fully confess and forsake any areas God brings to mind. Trust God to fill and empower you by His Spirit. After each of the following questions, pause to listen for God's impressions. (a) Am I lukewarm about spiritual things? ___ (b) Am I in any way proud or condescending toward others? ___ (c) Is there anyone about whom I think jealous, envious thoughts? ___ (d) Do I have an attitude of doubt and unbelief? ___ (e) Do I have any tendency toward being harsh or critical? Believe Christ to live through you by the Holy Spirit. (Romans 6:11) Put off wrong attitudes and let the mind of Christ dwell in you.

3. **Holy Speech** — *"But I say to you that for every idle word men may speak, they will give account of it in the day of judgment."* (Matthew 12:36) *"Let no corrupt communication proceed out of your mouth, but what is good for necessary edification, that it may impart grace to the hearers. ...Neither filthiness nor foolish talking, nor coarse jesting which are not fitting; but rather giving of thanks."* (Ephesians 4:29, 5:4) *"In everything give thanks: for this is the will of God in Christ Jesus concerning you."* (1 Thessalonians 5:18)

Fully confess and forsake any sins of speech. Trust God to fill and empower you by His Spirit. After each of the following questions, pause and allow God to speak. (a) Have I uttered any inappropriate or slang speech? ___ (b) Do I have patterns of cursing or off-color words? ___ (c) Am I prone to exaggeration or lying? ___ (d) Do I have patterns of complaining and griping? ___ (e) Am I guilty of any form of divisive speech? ___ (f) Do I have any patterns of critical, judgmental speech? ___ (g) Have I said things when alone that would cause great shame if made public? (Yet remember, all will be revealed). Believe Christ to live through you by the Holy Spirit. (Romans 6:11) Put off all ungodly speech and yield your tongue to Christ's Lordship.

4. **Right Relationships** — *"Therefore if you bring your gift to the altar, and there remember that your brother has something against you, leave your gift there before the altar, and go your way. First be reconciled to your brother, and then come and offer your gift...For if you forgive men their trespasses, your heavenly Father will also forgive you; but if you forgive not men their trespasses, neither will your Father forgive your trespasses."* (Matthew 5:23-24, 6:14-15)

Fully confess and forsake all relationship sins. Take your time and be thorough! After each of the following questions, pause and allow God to speak. (a) Is there anyone I have offended but have not asked forgiveness? ___ (b) Have I failed to seek full reconciliation and make restitution to anyone I have offended or harmed? ___ (c) Do I harbor the slightest unforgiveness and anger toward anyone? ___ (d) As a father, am I leading my family spiritually? ___ (e) As a mother, am I sacrificially and joyfully serving my family? ___ (f) Have I in any way failed to honor, respect or show attention to my parents? ___ (g) Have I spoken, emailed or texted negatively about anyone behind their back? ___ (h) Am I involved in any form of gossip or negative, critical speech? ___ Do I have unscriptural patterns in social media? ___ (i) Is there any pattern of failing to respect and support my spiritual leaders? Put off sins of relationship and let Jesus be the Lord of all.

5. **Rejecting Sins of Commission** — *"For I acknowledge my transgressions; and my sin is ever before me."* (Psalms 51:3)

Fully confess and forsake all sins of commission. After each of the following questions, pause for God to speak. (a) Am I engaged in any form of sexual immorality? ___ (b) Have I compromised by viewing anything unclean via movies, TV or Internet? ___ (c) Do I have habits that abuse or neglect my body? ___ (d) Do I commit idolatry by placing anyone or anything over loving and serving God? ___ (e) Have I dabbled in any form of gambling or new ageism? ___ (f) Am I doing anything for which I do not have perfect peace? ___ (g) Am I in any way harsh or unkind to others? ___ (h) Have I abused God's grace by taking sin lightly? ___ (i) Do I confess sins but fail to forsake them? Put off disobedience and put on full surrender to Christ.

6. **Renouncing Sins of Omission** — *"Therefore to him that knows to do good and does not do it, to him it is sin."* (James 4:17)

Fully confess and forsake any patterns of omission. After each of the following questions, pause and listen for God's impressions. (a) Am I failing to abide in Jesus by neglecting regular time in His Word and prayer? ___ (b) Do I neglect to be a daily witness and fail to generously support evangelism and missions? ___ (c) Have I neglected to discern and use my spiritual gifts? ___ (d) Am I allowing any point of spiritual bondage to remain in my life? ___ (e) Have I failed to support and respect my spiritual leaders? ___ (f) Am I failing to daily pursue holiness? ___ (g) Am I robbing God by failing to tithe and give generous offerings beyond the tithe? ___ (h) Have I neglected to work at improving my marriage and family life? ___ (i) Do I fail to pray with my family? Believe Christ to live through you by the Holy Spirit. (Romans 6:11) Put off sins of neglect and put on full obedience.

7. **Embracing Full Surrender and Obedience to Jesus** — *"If anyone desires to come after Me, let him deny himself and take up his cross, and follow Me."* (Matthew 16:24)

Fully confess and forsake whatever God reveals. After each of the following questions, pause for God to speak. (a) Have you willfully failed to surrender every part of your life to God's total control? ___ (b) Has God told you to do something yet you still haven't obeyed Him? ___ (c) Is there some area where you pretend not to know what God is saying, yet deep down you know you do? ___ (d) Are there things God has told you to stop; yet you still do them? ___ (e) Is there any area of service you should be doing; yet you are not? ___ (f) Have you continued to sin willfully in areas about which God has clearly spoken? Believe Christ to live through you by the Holy Spirit. (Romans 6:11) Put off self-will and wholly surrender to Christ's Lordship.

Drawing Near to God in Full Confidence
"Claim the Fullness of God's Spirit"

Once you have sincerely confessed your sins and yielded to Christ's Lordship, He promises to draw near and fill you with Himself. *"Draw near to God, and he will draw near to you."* (James 4:8) With cleansed hearts and fervent prayer you can indeed stand firm in God's wonderful promise of mercy and prayer.

Though we are all imperfect, His grace is greater than our weakness. *"If My people, which are called by My name, will humble themselves, and pray, and seek My face, and turn from their wicked ways; then I will hear from heaven, and will forgive their sin, and will heal their land."* (2 Chronicles 7:14) In these crucial days of destiny, may God find believers cleansed, yielded and praying for America. Remember, it is the prayers of clean hearts that avail much! (Psalm 24:3, 66:18; James 5:16)

After the step of consistent cleaning, there is yet one other step that releases God's incredible power for breakthrough. This second step involves the awesome power of united prayers of agreement. (Matthew 18:19; Acts 2:1, 4:31-32) A united prayer blitz has enormous breakthrough power for individuals, churches and families. Prayerfully consider "Step Two for Greater Power."

Step Two for Greater Power and Breakthrough
"Embrace a Prayer Blitz of United Agreement"
(Acts 1:14, 2:1; 2 Corinthians 10:3-5; James 5:16)

One of the most powerful principles for breakthrough is the biblical dynamic of united prayer. Another term is "praying together in one accord." (Acts 1:14, 2:1) Tragically, this unparalleled power is often neglected by individuals and couples. Yet there is good news in the fact united prayer is simple to embrace. A process I call the "united prayer blitz" combines several principles in one dynamic process.

The following process is the God-given path to spiritual warfare and breakthroughs. *It is how we go to war for our loved ones!* In over thirty years of ministry, I know of countless miraculous breakthroughs in couples and individuals who embraced a prayer blitz of united agreement. In many cases, they had tried everything else and their situations seemed hopeless. God has made incredible promises about the power of intense prayer, fasting and united agreement. (Jeremiah 29:12-13; Matthew 17:20-21; 18:19; Acts 1:14, 2:1; James 5:16)

Yes sadly, it is troubling how many modern believers are not taught the vital principles of united prayer, fasting and claiming God-given promises. Though these patterns are essential elements of spiritual warfare, many have not taken these simple steps for their loved ones. While these steps are neither magic nor guarantee quick answers, they are biblical and powerful for the demolishing of strongholds. By the biblical steps listed below, all believers can (and should) go to another level of power.

A Practical Process for Prayer Blitz Breakthroughs

1. The couple agrees to dedicate a certain period of time to give special focus to praying together for needed breakthroughs. The specified period can be a few days, a period of weeks or as long as they feel God's leading. The principle is to let

God guide and not to view this as a program. I suggest a period of at least three months of intensified focus.

2. It is vitally important to embrace *thorough* spiritual cleansing at the beginning (and throughout) the special period of prayer focus. We must not underestimate the importance of praying with cleansed hearts. In many ways, deep spiritual cleansing is the single biggest factor in dynamic, faith-filled praying. (Psalm 66:18; James 5:16)

3. Couples may agree to utilize fasting. One method is to miss the noon meal and give that time to prayer. Spirit-led fasting is often a powerful tool for increasing the impact of prayer. (Matthew 17:20-21; Mark 9:29) While we should never view fasting as legalism to "earn" God's favor, it is a point of obedience. Jesus never said "*if* you fast," He said "*when*." (Matthew 6:16)

4. Many couples ask others to join them in praying for their specific need during the specified time of focus. A practical approach is to ask them to take a moment to pray for your need at certain times of the day (i.e. breakfast, lunch, bedtime, etc.) It is important to consider prayerfully who you ask to join you in the united prayer blitz.

   In securing prayer partners, two principles are critical. (a) Ask people who will keep their commitment and (b) secure people whose prayers have power. Your prayer blitz will only be as powerful as the prayers and faithfulness of those who are in it!

5. It is especially powerful when couples make a commitment to meet periodically for corporate prayer with their prayer partners. Regular meetings also add the element of accountability. The meetings can be weekly or as often as agreed. There is enormous power in such united agreement! (Matthew 18:19; Acts 2:1; etc.) Jonathan Edwards called it

"explicit agreement" and "visible union" in "extraordinary prayer."

6. As the prayer blitz proceeds, ask God for promises and Scriptures to guide your praying. Ask God to increase and strengthen your faith. Praying God's revealed promises brings vastly increased power and faith into our intercession. We should also seek God's wisdom in identifying and tearing down specific strongholds in those for whom we are praying. (2 Corinthians 10:3-5) Ask the Lord to deliver and transform those we lift in one accord. (Matthew 6:13; Acts 12:5-12)

7. Don't give up! Persistence is an often neglected principle in breakthrough praying. (Matthew 18:1-9, 11:5-8) Great victories frequently require significant time and fervency. In Hebrews 6:12, the biblical writer says, "faith *and* patience inherit the promises." Many major breakthroughs take months and years. *Do not* be condemned or discouraged if you do not see quick results. While we should pray consistently, there are times God directs to an intensified united focus. Trust God for sensitivity to know when a united prayer blitz is needed. Also, ask for wisdom about any actions or steps you need to take beyond just prayer.

   Be further aware the nature of spiritual battle is to sometimes see things get worse before they get better. Because we are not *"wrestling against flesh and blood,"* the enemy may try to intensify his hold when he senses the Lord is dealing with a person's heart. While this does not always happen, do not be surprised or disheartened if it does. The devil may respond to your intensified effort with an intensified effort of his own. Always remember — Jesus is Lord and the enemy is defeated! Let us ever keep our eyes on Jesus, not our problems. (Hebrews 12:2)

Conclusion
A Personal Word of Encouragement

In our day, spiritual assault on marriages and families is at levels seldom seen in history. On every hand we hear stories of spiritual disaster. Yet, even now we are also hearing something else. More and more families are not only learning to pray, they are embracing prayer that is effective, fervent and united. (James 5:16) They are experiencing the awesome dynamic of praying a hedge of protection around themselves and their loved ones. Even more, they are learning to walk in true intimacy and power with the Savior. Make no mistake — Jesus is still on the throne and His power moves mountains.

Dear reader, I know your pressures and problems may seem overwhelming. Perhaps you've been praying but your mountains just aren't moving. Don't give up! Through the cleansing and practical principles in this tool, you will experience a major difference if you persist. Above all, you will be learning to seek God's face, not just His hand. Rather than viewing prayer as merely a way to get answers, you will view it as the means of knowing God and being changed into His image. (2 Corinthians 3:18) And always remember this comforting truth — if you take five sincere steps toward God in deeper prayer, He will often take fifty toward you!

Believers, when you find greater closeness and intimacy with Jesus, you find everything! Please know that God loves you more than words could ever express. I close with three wonderful words and promises from God Himself. *"And ye shall seek me, and find me, when ye shall search for me with all your heart."* (Jeremiah 29:13) *"Draw near to God and He will draw near to you."* (James 4:8a) *"The effective, fervent prayer of a righteous man avails much."* (James 5:16b)

Suggested Resources

As foundational guides to growth and power in Christ, I suggest readers study **How to Develop a Powerful Prayer Life** and **Returning to Holiness** or **Return to Me**. Each of these books provide deeper insights and practical patterns for phenomenal intimacy and power in Christ.

Many groups also greatly benefit from church or regional conference entitled, *Going Deeper With God*. In this conference, individuals and churches experience powerful revival in prayer, spiritual awakening and family renewal. We now include an emphasis on individual and family breakthroughs.

For Resources or Conference Inquiries Contact:

Dr. Gregory Frizzell
3800 N. May Ave
Oklahoma City, OK 73112
405.942.3000 x4517
gfrizzell@bgco.org

Or

Dr. Gregory Frizzell
11317 Twisted Oak Rd.
Oklahoma City, OK 73120
405.990.3730
gfrizzell@earthlink.net

Or

http://frizzellministries.org

Appendix A

My Prayer Covenant for Revival and Spiritual Awakening

With morals collapsing and judgment rising, it is essential that God's millions unite in the effective, fervent prayer of clean hearts. (2 Chronicles 7:14; Matthew 18:19; James 5:16) There is enormous power when believers covenant together in fervent, united prayer and repentance! Yet it is also vital that we pray with biblical depth and effectiveness. The following prayers are both biblical and complete in reflecting God's heart. Prayerfully adopt the following covenant. **I covenant with God and millions of saints to pray these prayers until God *"rends the heavens."*** (Isaiah 64:1)

Seven Covenant Prayers for Revival and Spiritual Awakening

1. Pray for God to have *mercy* and move believers to true *brokenness in acknowledging His righteous judgment* (2 Chronicles 7:14; Jeremiah 29:13)

2. Pray for *love, repentance* and *holy reverential fear* to grip God's people (Matthew 22:37-39; 2 Corinthians 7:1)

3. Pray for a spirit of bold *faith* and *intercession* to fill believers (Matthew 21:13; Acts 2:1; Hebrews 11:6)

4. Pray for *holiness, boldness* and *power* in God's leaders and churches (Acts 1:8; 1 Corinthians 2:4)

5. Pray for *loving unity* and *oneness* to engulf Christ's Church (John 13:34; Acts 2:42-47)

6. Pray for burning *passion* and *power* in evangelism and missions (Matthew 28:18-20; Acts 1:8)

7. Pray for God to "*rend the heavens*" in *sweeping revival* and *spiritual awakening* (2 Chronicles 7:14; Isaiah 64:1; Psalm 85:6)

"If My people who are called by My name will humble themselves, and pray and seek My face, and turn from their wicked ways, then I will hear from heaven, and will forgive their sin and heal their land." (2 Chronicles 7:14)

"Will You not revive us again, That Your people may rejoice in You? Show us Your mercy, LORD, And grant us Your salvation." (Psalm 85:6-7)

"Oh, that You would rend the heavens! That You would come down! That the mountains might shake at Your presence." (Isaiah 64:1)

Appendix B

My Covenant to Pray for the Lost
Transforming Loved Ones and Neighbors

"The effective, fervent prayer of the righteous is powerful."
(James 5:16b)

Dear Father, because you have commanded us to witness to all the world and make disciples, I start with my family and loved ones. ***By Your grace, I covenant to do five things***. (1) I will daily embrace Your cleansing, fullness and power. (2) I will pray for myself and my church to have a missional focus and aggressively witness to all the world. (3) I will fervently pray for my list of lost souls and ever seek ways to bring them to Christ. (4) I will seek to be a daily witness wherever I go. (5) I will give sacrificially to evangelism and missions.

Souls I Covenant to Lift to God

_____

_____

_____

_____

_____

_____

_____

_____

_____

_____

_____

How to Effectively Pray for the Lost

✟ Pray for their hearts to be *deeply convicted of sin* and lostness (John 16:8)

✟ Pray for God to *open their eyes* and *reveal Christ* as Lord and Savior (Matthew 16:17; 2 Corinthians 4:4)

✟ Pray for them to be overwhelmingly *drawn to Christ* by God's Spirit (John 6:44)

✟ Pray for God to *tear down any barriers* keeping them from salvation (2 Corinthians 10:15)

✟ Pray for God to make their hearts *good soil* fully receptive to Christ (Matthew 13:8)

✟ Pray for God to grant them the *new birth* and *true repentance* (2 Corinthians 5:17; Luke 13:3)

✟ Pray that they *become fruitful disciples* that lead others to Christ (Matthew 28:18-20; John 15:8)

Appendix C

My Covenant for Prayers that Protect and Transform My Family

Recognizing that the first responsibility to my loved ones is spiritual,

Recognizing that effective prayer is essential to their spiritual protection and transformation,

Recognizing that God's grace is sufficient for me to pray in power.

Recognizing that God has provided Powerful Prayer for Every Family as a simple Bible-filled tool and personal journal for effective prayer

I hereby covenant to teach my children the essential truths of Scripture.

I covenant to pray and record specific prayers of protection for the major areas of their lives,

I covenant to pray and record specific prayers of transformation for the major areas of their lives.

I covenant to identify specific biblical prayers and claim specific promises for my loved ones.

I covenant to seek ever-deepening empowerment in my own life and prayers.

I covenant to embrace one accord prayer, fasting and spiritual warfare when I sense attacks on my children or spouse.

While I know I will not be perfect, I trust God's grace to bless and empower my efforts.

To God and Christ be all glory and praise.

_____   _____
Signed   Dated

Key Prayers and Promises for Loved Ones
My Journal of Faith and Transformation
(Mark 11:22-24; Hebrews 6:12)

Scriptures Claimed for   *Key Biblical Prayers*

_____   _____

_____   _____

_____   _____

_____   _____

_____   _____

_____   _____

_____   _____

_____   _____

_____   _____

_____   _____

_____   _____

_____   _____

_____   _____

_____   _____

_____   _____

Scriptures Claimed for   *Key Biblical Prayers*

_____   _____

_____   _____

_____   _____

_____   _____

_____   _____

_____   _____

_____   _____

_____   _____

_____   _____

_____   _____

_____   _____

_____   _____

_____   _____

_____   _____

_____   _____

_____   _____

_____   _____

_____   _____

_____   _____

_____   _____

_____   _____

_____   _____

_____   _____

_____   _____

_____   _____

If God has touched you through this material, please consider partnering with us to touch the world!

The Restored Foundations Initiative
A Strategic Vision for Revival and Global Evangelism

The Restored Foundation Initiative is a global strategy of Gregory Frizzell Ministries, Inc. It involves a strategic three year project to powerfully impact two to three million people. The project targets two to three million people internationally. The objective is to restore key revival, empowered evangelism, healthy church planting, small groups and biblical discipleship.

Based on historic patterns, this is the type of saturation that is essential for a major spiritual awakening. Currently, nothing of this strategic nature or size is being done. Because of a unique arrangement with Bethany International Publishers, our ministry has the capability of accomplishing this far-reaching book distribution at very low cost. We are seeking individual believers, business leaders and churches to partner in this global initiative for sweeping revival, spiritual awakening and missions. Targeted projects are available for churches or individuals to adopt for particular groups for impact. We are praying for partners in funding and prayer.

THE RESTORED FOUNDATIONS INITIATIVE

If you are interested in further details or would like to participate in this project, please see the information below.

Contact Information: Dr. Gregory R. Frizzell, 11317 Twisted Oak Rd., Oklahoma City, OK 73120; gfrizzell@bgco.org or gfrizzell@earthlink.net;
405-990-3730 or 405-752-0782